No Comment

Vintage Books

A DIVISION OF RANDOM HOUSE

New York

No Comment

Edited by Erwin Knoll

Illustrated by
Stuart Goldenberg

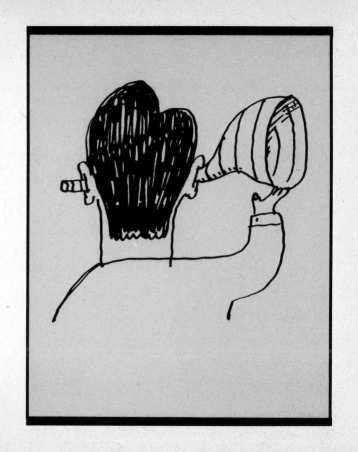

A Vintage Original, October 1984
First Edition

Published in the United States by Random House, Inc.,
New York, and simultaneously in Canada by
Random House of Canada Limited, Toronto.

Library of Congress Cataloging in Publication Data
No comment.
A compendium compiled by the Progressive magazine.
1. Wit and humor. I. Knoll, Erwin. II. Goldenberg,
Stuart. III. Progressive magazine (New York, N.Y.)
PN6153.N6   1984   818′.54′08   84-40001
ISBN 0-394-72559-X (pbk.)

Manufactured in the United States of America
Book design: Iris Weinstein

Preface

The story appeared one recent Tuesday morning in the New York *Times.* It was datelined Livermore, California, and it began:

> Behind fences topped with barbed wire and doors equipped with combination locks, dozens of young physicists and engineers at the Lawrence National Laboratory work late into the night, six and seven days a week, on classified projects aimed at creating the next generation of nuclear weapons. Their dream, they say, is to end the nuclear arms race.

"I'll be damned," I said, and reached for the scissors. It was another clipping for the NO COMMENT file.

Why NO COMMENT? Well, what is there to say?

What would *you* say if you read in a Baton Rouge, Louisiana, newspaper about a man who cut the corners off a $20 bill and pasted them on a $1 bill to make a bogus $20 bill? The judge who sentenced him called him "the most inept counterfeiter I ever heard of"—but was his comment really necessary?

Is there any need to analyze the news that in the event of nuclear attack, civil defense officials in Utica, New York, plan to order 1,000 hamburgers and 1,000 cups of coffee from carry-out restaurants to sustain the occupants of fallout shelters?

Must anything more be said about President Reagan's solemn warning to campaign workers in Las Vegas that his re-election drive required "mouth-to-mouth, hand-to-hand contact"?

I suppose one could write an editorial, an essay, or even a doctoral dissertation about the small-arms dealer in Nashville, Tennessee, who advertised .38-caliber pistols as "a lasting gift of love" for Valentine's Day—and sold a couple of dozen at $214.95 each. But why bother?

Every day, newspapers across the country carry stories that offer powerful evidence of rampant and pervasive lunacy. Sometimes those stories are played prominently on the front page—a headline, for example, in Lima, Ohio: REAGAN HELPS SLING SANDBAGS; FLOODS WORSEN. More often, they are small items, buried back among the truss ads—like the announcement in the *Star-Tribune* of Casper, Wyoming, that an Eagle Scout would lecture on "terrorism operations and how we all fit in."

As editor of *The Progressive,* I've been collecting these gems of luminous inanity for the past ten years. Readers of our magazine send them in from all over the country, and every month we publish a dozen or so of the best. The rule is that they must speak for themselves—and, in the case of this book, that they must stand the test of time.

When you assemble about two hundred NO COMMENT items in one volume, you begin to form an interesting picture of America. You might call it Exhibit A in a petition to certify a whole nation as deranged. You might, but I won't. I'll just say: NO COMMENT.

ERWIN KNOLL
Madison, Wisconsin

No Comment

■ Buckle Up

The Georgia State Senate voted 29 to 22 to approve a "traveling electric chair" that would move from county to county to execute condemned offenders. Said Senator Ronnie Walker, "Folks read about the electric chair, they hear about it —but those folks with criminal minds don't care about the law. But if they see that chair moving down the highway, it might save a life."

■ Child Pornography

Novelist Kay Boyle obtained her security files under the Freedom of Information Act and found in the almost 2,000 pages of dossiers the assertion that she "had a clandestine affair with Ezra Pound before World War I." Her comment: "I would have been no more than ten— and I didn't like him then."

■ A Brand-New Ball Game

A U.S. military adviser in El Salvador who formerly served in Vietnam, Cambodia, Laos and Thailand, as quoted in the New York *Times:* "All I want to do is win one war, that's all, just one. It'll be like winning the World Series for me."

■ Fore

Martel Lovelace, an official of the National Rifle Association, said a gun is "a recreational tool, like a golf club or a tennis racket. You can kill someone with a golf club, you know."

■ Perfectly Clear

President Reagan on civil defense, as quoted in Robert Scheer's book *With Enough Shovels: Reagan, Bush & Nuclear War:* "I think we're going to have to start a civil defense program. I think—see, they violated and we kept to the premise that McNamara, in the original getting together and what resulted in our doing away with our antiballistic missile system, at a time when we were ahead of them in technology on that."

■ Hymns for Gyms

National Catholic Reporter says business is booming for Christian aerobic-exercise record albums bearing such titles as *Believercise, Firm Believer, Message in Motion* and *Aerobic Glow.*

■ Draft Dodger

Received at Disneyland—a letter from the Selective Service System addressed to "Mickey M. Mouse" and opening with these words: "Dear Registrant: Our records indicate you have not responded to our initial request for necessary date-of-birth information. . . ."

■ The Answer Is Yes

The FBI is opening dossiers on citizens who write
to the FBI to ask whether it is keeping dossiers
on them.

■ Birds of No Feathers

U.S. Department of Agriculture researchers at Beltsville, Maryland, are producing featherless chickens. The birds tend to be nervous and develop stomach ulcers. They run around a lot, trying to keep warm.

■ Spirit of '76

The Pennsylvania Bicentennial Commission had second thoughts about its plan to invite citizens to rededicate themselves to American ideals by signing copies of the Declaration of Independence. "If you sit down and read it," said George Ebner, the commission's executive director, "you'll find it's a pretty revolutionary document. There may be a lot of people unwilling to sign it."

■ Out From Under

Roberto Monsivais of Mexico City invented an emergency alarm called a "life detector." It summons help for those who find they have been given premature funerals.

■ Identity Crisis

When an undercover police officer in Omaha, Nebraska, appeared in court wearing a gorilla mask to conceal his identity while testifying in a narcotics case, police officials ordered him to switch to a pillowcase disguise to preserve "an aura of professionalism."

■ Vote Now, Ask Later

The workings of the World's Greatest Deliberative Body, as perceived by Senator Russell B. Long, Louisiana Democrat: "If every man insists on knowing what he's voting for before he votes, we're not going to get a bill reported before Monday."

■ Die Now, Pay Later

Eight years after Arthur T. Aldridge died, leaving a widow and three children, his tombstone in Boston's Union Cemetery was repossessed because a $70 payment was overdue.

■ Use Only As Directed

The New York Department of Mental Hygiene produced and distributed a three-page illustrated memorandum on how to split an English muffin.

■ Why Uncle Sam Wants You

From the "Fashions of The Times" supplement to the New York *Times:* "Ever since Joan of Arc, the sight of a woman in martial gear has continued to produce a shiver not entirely attributable to patriotism. . . . When a woman puts on a uniform, she appears to set aside her interest in the pervasive flux of meaning and feeling and to opt suddenly for strict rules. The immediate effect can be quite erotic."

■ Frontiers of Agronomy

Walton C. Galinat, a research professor of genetics at the University of Massachusetts, developed a square ear of sweet corn "so it won't roll off the plate."

■ Stuff and Mount

Cowboy star Roy Rogers offered his own design for immortality: "When my time comes, I want Dale to skin me and put me right up there on Trigger."

■ Hamburger Helper

The late General Creighton Abrams, quoted in *Dollars & Sense:* "It's good for a young person to work at McDonald's. It makes you an efficient person. If you make the wrong size hamburger, you get fired. It is a smooth-running machine that the Army should emulate."

■ The Jeweler's Eye

Tiffany & Co., the Fifth Avenue diamond merchants, asked the federal government (in a New York *Times* advertisement) to "stop persecuting God."

■ Spirit of '84

Beulah Easton of Bloomington, Illinois, was sentenced to pay a $50 fine for criminal trespass after distributing copies of the Declaration of Independence at a shopping center.

■ Military Science

The U.S. Army transferred Sergeant Major Jimmy A. Powell from his ROTC duties at Northern Michigan University after he bit the head off a live chicken and drank the bird's blood during a military-science class. Powell's commanding officer said such actions were appropriate for field survival training but not for the classroom.

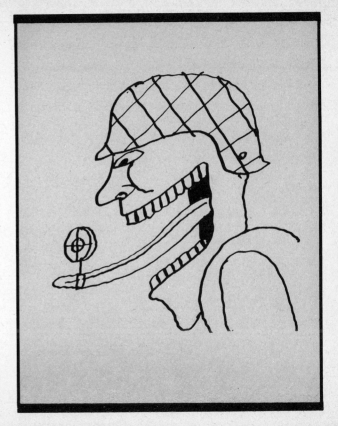

■ With Friends Like These . . .

As "a show of confidence" in the Salvadoran economy, Bristol-Myers de Centroamerica is introducing a hair dye called Clairesse. A Bristol-Myers spokesman explained: "We're not just interested in business, we also want to take part in reactivating the country."

■ Language in Action

S. I. Hayakawa, semanticist and Republican senator from California, commenting on the Panama Canal: "We should keep it. After all, we stole it fair and square."

■ Soda Pop

A Dayton, Ohio, judge declared a mistrial when two bottles of Pepsi-Cola exploded in his courtroom. The bottles had been entered as exhibits in a $500,000 damage suit filed by a man who claimed to have been injured by an exploding Pepsi-Cola bottle.

■ Political Proliferation

Walter Mondale, explaining why Democrats outnumber Republicans: "We are more handsome, we are happier, we are warmer, we are sexier, and we have more kids."

■ Bring Back the Stork

Phyllis Schlafly says sex education is "a principal cause of teen-age pregnancy."

■ Subject to Change

From a memorandum issued by the Office of Management and Budget: "An agency subject to the provisions of the Federal Reports Act may enter into an arrangement with an organization not subject to the Act whereby the organization not subject to the Act collects information on behalf of the agency subject to the Act. The reverse also occurs."

■ Being and Nothingness

When press dispatches from Paris reported in June 1964 that Jean-Paul Sartre had joined the "Who Killed Kennedy Committee,"
J. Edgar Hoover sprang into action. According to FBI documents, the Director promptly scribbled a memo: "Find out who Sartre is."

■ The Smoking Gum

A nicotine chewing gum designed to help smokers give up the habit was withdrawn from the market in Sweden after researchers found that children used the gum, got hooked on nicotine and then switched to cigarettes.

■ Thou Shalt Kill

From a discussion of capital punishment in *United Evangelic Action,* the official organ of the National Association of Evangelicals: "The highest function of government is the judicial taking of life. All other government powers are implied in that. The death penalty also reflects the seriousness with which God regards sin."

■ Pay As You Go

Florida State Senator Lori Wilson, explaining her forthright opposition to pay toilets: "If God had meant for us to have pay toilets, we would have been born with exact change."

■ Means Without End

David Ogilvy, founder of the Ogilvy and Mather advertising agency, addressing members of the Dallas Advertising League: "In the course of defining the purpose of your corporate advertising, it is often necessary to define the purpose of the corporation, and—you know this—most corporations don't have any purpose."

■ Levi's as Levelers

Texas Agriculture Commissioner Reagan Brown, defeated for re-election in the Democratic primary, on the desirability of having everyone wear blue jeans: "You couldn't tell the Jews and the Texans apart. If we could get blue jeans on everyone in the world, we would have world peace."

■ A Penny Saved

The Internal Revenue Service sent a registered letter to Lloyd Rummer advising him that his company, Empire Auto Parts, in Colville, Washington, owed the government one cent.

■ The Glow of Good Health

In a teaching manual prepared for use in public schools, the Federal Emergency Management Agency compared the radiation released by a nuclear blast to sunlight: "Long exposure in one day can be harmful, while the same total exposure distributed over a few weeks produces a nice tan."

■ Love, American Style

The Zero Population Growth Foundation of Washington, D.C., designated February 14 as "Love Carefully Day" and distributed Valentine cards emblazoned with red condoms.

■ It's Not the Gift That Counts, It's the Sediment Behind It

The Burlington Northern Railroad transferred to the U.S. Government a square-mile parcel at the top of the Mount St. Helens volcano in the state of Washington. Announcing the gift in a letter to President Reagan, Chairman Richard M. Bressler of the Burlington Northern wrote: "It is our hope that this donation will encourage the careful management of the St. Helens area for the contemplation and enjoyment of future generations."

■ No Sacrifice Too Great

The Consolidated Edison Co. of New York announced it was "trimming the fat from the budget" by removing linen towels from its executive washrooms.

■ Onward, Christian Soldiers

The Reverend Earl Johnson, minister of Christ Lutheran Church in San Lorenzo, California, had his crucifix confiscated when he was arrested in an antiwar demonstration. "It might be used as a weapon," he was told.

■ Job Description

A Pentagon brochure advising retiring military personnel on how to prepare a job résumé included the following sample entry for a Navy pilot who flew bombing missions in Southeast Asia: ". . . located profitable areas for the concentration of resources. . . ."

■ Sure Thing

A White House official, assuring the *Wall Street Journal* that Ronald Reagan would definitely seek a second term: "If there's one thing we're certain of, it's our certitudes."

■ 10-4, Good Buddy

Mounce Brady Jackson, known on the CB channels in Southern California as Big Moose, died in an auto accident and received a CB funeral. The Reverend George A. Wood of the Lemon Heights Baptist Church of Orange eulogized the departed as an example of how "the Great Broadcaster plugs you into his power and modulates through you," and consoled mourners with the thought that Big Moose was not really gone—"He's just out of range."

■ Green-Collar Crime

Girl Scout officials found it necessary to crack down on mothers who pocketed the proceeds of cookie sales.

■ A Word to the Wise

Former Under Secretary of State George C. McGhee, writing in the *Foreign Service Journal:* "I believe, with a few exceptions, that Foreign Service officers have a genuine desire to help our companies. Those who take an indifferent or superior attitude will not, I believe, accede to higher posts. . . . Let's all get down to multinational business."

■ Let Them Dig Shelters

The U.S. Fish and Wildlife Service agreed to let the Air Force use almost 75 percent of the Desert National Wildlife Range in Nevada for bombing exercises. "We feel we will still have control over the area," said Bob Yoder of the Wildlife Service. "We feel the animals are in safe hands."

■ Let 'em Eat Crabmeat

When a Chicago woman who raises two handicapped sons wrote to President Reagan to protest budget cutbacks in funds for educating the handicapped, the White House sent her two eight-by-ten glossy photos of the Reagans, a form letter on voluntarism, and a recipe for crabmeat casserole.

■ Nature Adores a Vacuum

Michael Eberhardt, director of the Defense Department's Office of Criminal Investigations, Policy and Oversight, told the New York *Times* that a new investigative unit would "fill a sorely needed vacuum."

■ We'll Drink to That

The lower house of the Alabama Legislature approved a bill raising the legal drinking age from nineteen to fifty.

■ Or Put to Sleep

Mayor Donald Master of Charles Town, West Virginia, a veterinarian: "These bleeding hearts, mothers that you read about in the Washington *Post* . . . they've got twelve kids and no father. They should have been spayed ten kids ago."

■ The Power of Positive Thinking

Two electric co-ops in Minnesota, the United Power Association of Elk River and the Cooperative Power Association of Minneapolis, earmarked up to $300,000 for a nine-month study of alleged adverse health effects along high-voltage power lines "to confirm our belief that these lines pose no adverse health effects."

■ Short-Footed Dogs

Advertising Age advised its readers that "according to National Hot Dog and Sausage Council rules, the term 'foot-long' may be applied to any frank that exceeds eight inches."

■ Discontented Cows

Agrophysics, Inc., of San Francisco, marketed a plastic intrauterine device for heifers, so that they can gain weight without "energy-wasting sexual behavior."

■ Dirty Duck

The city council of Helsinki, Finland, canceled library subscriptions to Donald Duck comic books, citing his fifty-year engagement to Daisy Duck and other indications of a racy life style from which children should be shielded.

■ The Sporting Life

Dorf/MJH, a public relations firm, advised its corporate clients to attract media coverage by sponsoring "unusual, offbeat, and lesser-known sports—such as floor hockey, caber tossing, and walking on water."

■ Pipe-Downable

A spokesman for Consolidated Freightways, Inc., of San Francisco, told the *Wall Street Journal* that capital spending in the trucking industry "tends to fluctuate widely because much of our spending is very deferrable and quickly crank-upable."

■ Theirs Not to Reason Why . . .

General John A. Wickham Jr., the U.S. Army Chief of Staff, on the superior quality of today's soldiers: "They are the best in my thirty-three years of service. They'll fight, and they are as patriotic as you or I. They follow orders, and they die."

■ . . . Theirs But to Do and Die

A U.S. military adviser in El Salvador, as quoted by Charles Mohr in the New York *Times:* "To a civilian it may sound strange, but one encouraging sign is that the second lieutenants are starting to die out there. That means they are making mistakes and their own mistakes are killing them, but they are leading men and being aggressive."

■ Masterpiece Theater It Ain't

Herbert Schmertz, vice president for public affairs of Mobil Oil, explaining why Mobil (and other major corporate sponsors) declined to help fund a thirteen-hour public television documentary on the Vietnam war: "It's just not our thing. We do serial drama."

■ An Orange Is an Orange Is an Apple

President Reagan, responding to a press conference question: "I have always, kind of, held to a rule that until it is—I will talk about vetoes in general principle. But until it actually gets to my desk, I have always said that in the legislative process sometimes an orange becomes an apple. And I will wait and make that decision."

■ Edsel Died for Our Sins

At the weekly luncheon of the Detroit Economic Club, City Councilman David Eberhard offered the following prayer: "Almighty God, we thank Thee for the wheel. For the person who made it into a vehicle. For those who produce it. And bless us who use it. Amen."

■ Gab from the Grave

Stanley Zelazny, a manufacturing engineer in Sunnyvale, California, invented a solar-powered plexiglass "electronic tombstone" which broadcasts up to ninety minutes of pretaped messages in the voice of the deceased.

■ Frontiers of Communism

A footwear factory in Canton, People's Republic of China, produces fragrant shoes which, it claims, not only prevent sweating but "are also helpful in curing beriberi."

■ Take the A-Bomb

New York State Senator Martin M. Solomon, commenting on news that the New York City Transit Authority was looking into ways of protecting the subway system's power supply in the event of nuclear war: "The Transit Authority can't keep the trains rolling during an average rush hour. Why is it worrying about a nuclear attack?"

■ Good to the Last Drop

According to a Dow Chemical Company report, chloracne, the skin condition caused by exposure to dioxin, is "usually not disabling but may be fatal."

■ The Way We Were

Deep in a salt mine at Hutchinson, Kansas, vital artifacts and documents have been stored away for survivors of a nuclear holocaust—including hundreds of Metro-Goldwyn-Mayer movie negatives and the franchise records of Pizza Hut, Inc.

■ Now He Belongs to the Ages

Richard Nixon's presidency, as summed up by Watergate conspirator E. Howard Hunt in an interview with the *Herald-Tribune* of Sarasota, Florida: "The principal achievement of his Administration was that he avoided going to prison and he walked off with an awful lot of booty."

■ Baste Often for Best Results

The Hammacher Schlemmer department store in
New York City has a solar-powered lounge chair
which "rotates once every fifteen minutes for
more uniform tanning." It costs $4,500.

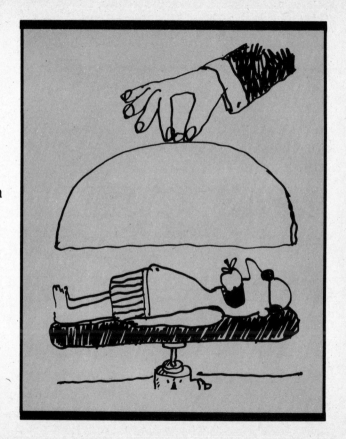

■ Such a Bargain

Police in Knoxville, Tennessee, arrested a couple for trying to swap their newborn daughter for a 25″ color television set.

■ Success Story

At the ripe old age of nineteen, Jimmy Johnson of Houston was elected to the exalted post of Grand Dragon of the Texas Fiery Knights of the Ku Klux Klan. He modestly attributed his success to a Dale Carnegie self-improvement course.

■ Two Wrongs Make a Right?

Robert P. Beasley, former executive vice president of Firestone Rubber Co., was indicted by a federal grand jury for allegedly stealing most of $1 million in corporate money that was intended for illegal political campaign contributions.

■ How to Spot a G-Man

"Years ago, all the FBI agents drank Yukon Jack," says Hal Binyon, owner of a bar and restaurant near Chicago's Federal Building. "Now they all drink wine spritzers."

■ Of Course and Certainly

J. Curtis McKay, a member of the Wisconsin State Elections Board: "I'm for abolishing and doing away with redundancy."

■ Danger of Democracy

Republican National Committeeman Van H. Archer Jr. opposed a plan to elect city council members in San Antonio, Texas, from residential districts because "when local government becomes too close to the people, it inevitably leads to corruption."

■ Renters' Revenge

The *Cash Newsletter* reported that an entrepreneur in Deemster, Arkansas, sells cockroaches to tenants who are vacating their apartments and have been asked by the landlord to leave the premises exactly as they found them.

■ Big (Though Belated) News for Vietnam Vets

News item from the Los Angeles *Times:* "NEW YORK—Do not wear green clothes in Southeast Asia, warns a consulting firm that advises U.S. businessmen on foreign protocol. The color is regarded as a sign of disease."

■ Comparative Literature

When the *Patriot-News* in Harrisburg, Pennsylvania, announced it would drop "Dick Tracy" because of excessive violence in the comic strip, creator Max Collins protested, "You might as well ban Shakespeare and the Bible."

■ Keep America Beautiful

Montana Power Company Chairman Joe McElwain, as quoted in the Portland *Oregonian:* "I happen to be one of those people who think the aesthetics of an area are improved by putting a nice transmission line through it."

■ New Ideas

Sam (Mr. Clean) Silverstein of Pittsburgh, Pennsylvania, advised the Federal Election Commission he was running for President on a platform that included abolishing Wednesday, decreasing the velocity of bullets by 98 percent, and eliminating the Postal Service deficit by issuing ten-cent stamps bearing nude photographs of famous Americans.

■ Good Neighbor

Dan R. Eddy Jr., a member of the Texas Good Neighbor Commission, a state agency devoted to promoting better understanding between Texas and Mexico, as quoted in the Texas *Observer:* "If I would never get to Mexico again it wouldn't bother me. I don't like the food or the climate."

■ Telling It Like It Is

Headline over an Associated Press story on the front page of the Lima (Ohio) *News:* REAGAN HELPS SLING SANDBAGS; FLOODS WORSEN.

■ Standin' in the Need of Prayer

Lieutenant Colonel Malcolm Brummitt, a United Church of Christ minister who served as the Pentagon's chaplain, observed, "It's a fantastic kind of ministry. . . . My calendar is usually very full every day. There is much work to be done here."

■ Let There Be Light

The General Accounting Office ascertained that the District of Columbia owns enough incandescent and mercury-vapor lights to last 561 years.

■ Keep 'em Unconfused

Retired General William C. Westmoreland, who commanded U.S. forces in Vietnam, said the next time America goes to war, the news media will have to be gagged. "Without censorship," he explained, "things can get terribly confused in the public mind."

■ Marketing Scents

Wham-O, a toy company in San Gabriel, California, announced that it mixes an artificial peppermint fragrance into its hula hoops. Wham-O also makes chocolate-scented Frisbees for dogs.

■ Why Children Fail

Principal Frank Braden of Dobie High School in Pasadena, Texas, barred fifteen-year-old Troy Erickson from classes because he wore an earring. When boys wear earrings, Braden explained, "this is instrumental in their not doing well in school."

■ Just the Facts

Lieutenant Robert Stark of the Indianapolis Police Department, national president of the Fraternal Order of Police, addressing the annual Police Appreciation Dinner of the Wheeling (West Virginia) Lions Club: "Don't get me wrong. I'm not saying all public officials are bad. But . . . our leaders are leftists, Communists, homosexuals, violent agitators, and members of the Trilateral Commission."

■ No Good Vibes

In London, a couple were denied the right to adopt a baby because their marriage "exuded excessive harmony" and would expose a child to insufficient "negative experiences."

■ Whitewright Is Ready

The municipality of Whitewright, Texas (pop. 1,743), used funds contributed by an anonymous donor to purchase four 9mm machine guns. Mayor Felix Robinson explained the weapons would come in handy in case of "riot or nuclear attack."

■ What to Do When They Get Uppity

The Georgia Chamber of Commerce invited business executives to a "strategy seminar for managing today's white-collar woman," promising advice on what to do when "female clerical employees barge in noisily" to state their grievances.

This One's for You

St. John Lutheran School in Lansing, Illinois, awarded a first prize in its Talent Festival to Jeff Nicklas and John Keidaisch for their outstanding collection of beer cans.

It's a Bird, It's a Plane . . .

News item from United Press International: "LANGLEY, VA.—Officials at Langley Air Force Base said today that a cannon that hurls dead chickens at airplanes at 700 miles an hour is helping to reduce accidents caused by jets hitting birds. Major Dennis Funnemark said the device, called a chicken gun, was a converted twenty-foot cannon that shoots four-pound chickens into the engines, windshields, and landing gear to determine how much damage such collisions can cause."

Interface

Security experts for a Japanese computer firm devised a means of barring unauthorized access: The computer recognizes the lip prints of authorized programmers.

■ The Pause That Refreshes

The San Francisco *Chronicle,* in an editorial praising Senate confirmation of Kenneth Adelman as director of the Arms Control and Disarmament Agency, commended Adelman for his "refreshingly frank admission" that he had never given much thought to the possibility of nuclear disarmament.

■ Splitting Hairs

The school board in Greenwood, Texas, barred a five-year-old boy from kindergarten because his hair came down below his ears. "You can't have a school without morals," a board member explained.

■ Progress in Peru

The military government of General Juan Velasco Alvarado closed two independent news magazines and expelled nine journalists as part of its campaign to "achieve a new society in which the Peruvian man and woman can have liberty and justice."

■ Big Mac Attack

In the event of nuclear attack, civil defense officials in Utica, New York, plan to order 1,000 hamburgers and 1,000 cups of coffee from carry-out restaurants to sustain occupants of municipal fallout shelters.

■ Peacekeeper

A man in Morgantown, West Virginia, admitted he had taken almost 1,900 college texts worth more than $60,000 from eight area libraries. He said the books contained information that could be used to design nuclear weapons, and he wanted to keep them from falling into the wrong hands.

■ In Cold Ink

President Reagan at the signing of the Social Security bill: "And I am now going over and sign, and as you can notice how cold it is, twelve pens there are too cold—they can only sign one letter, each pen. If my name came out to thirteen letters, I would have misspelled it."

■ Sawdust Sandwich

The Federal Trade Commission ordered the
Continental Baking Co., a subsidiary of
International Telephone and Telegraph, to explain
in its advertising that the "high fiber" in Fresh
Horizons bread consists of wood or tree pulp.

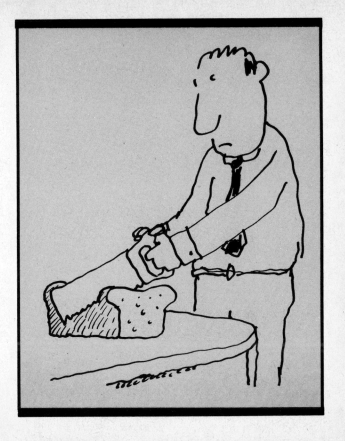

■ Beating Inflation

James B. Sanders of Baton Rouge, Louisiana, described by a federal judge as "the most inept counterfeiter I ever heard of," was sentenced to five years' probation for cutting the corners off a $20 bill and pasting them on a $1 bill to make a bogus $20 bill.

■ Mistaken Identity

Peggy Coquet of Portland, Oregon, wanted her representative in Congress to know she was opposed to any deal with Iran for release of American hostages, so she fired off a telegram: "Make no trades with thugs." Representative Les AuCoin, Oregon Democrat, replied: "Thank you for contacting me regarding the proposal to provide Government assistance to Chrysler."

■ Hi-Tech in Action

At the British Ford engine plant in South Wales, engineers spent three months and $360,000 to cope with occasional jams in the assembly line. The solution: an official kicker who wears a steel-toed boot and kicks the engine-bearing pallet when it stalls.

■ Sunset

High Country News reported that a solar-powered electric chair has been developed, though the $5,000 price tag "might seem a little steep, especially for smaller states."

■ First Things First

Question addressed to the "TV Q&A " column of *TV Guide* magazine: "If we become involved in a nuclear war, would the electromagnetic pulses from exploding bombs damage my videotapes? Should I store them in a lead-lined container?"

■ Wet Women Not Wanted

A U.S. Treasury Department official explained to the *Wall Street Journal* that only men were appointed to a forty-five-member savings bond sales committee because "this committee has always had a lot of prestige, and we haven't wanted to water down the membership."

■ They're Everywhere, They're Everywhere

Columnist Charley Reese in the *Union Leader* of Manchester, New Hampshire: "The Soviet Union has a powerful lobby in the United States which consists of Communists, socialists, greedy bankers and businessmen, pacifists, and cowards."

■ Peanuts and a Prize

John Iglesias of Santa Ana, California, found a miniature sex manual in a box of Cracker Jack. "I was shocked," he said. "I was thinking it was going to be little pages of cartoons or little paste-on tattoos." Borden, Inc., manufacturer of Cracker Jack, said it has instituted "extensive security measures."

■ Professional Standard

A bill to legalize prostitution in the state of Washington provided that licenses be issued "only upon satisfactory proof that the applicant is of good character."

■ Grand Opening

From the *Brazil Herald* of Rio de Janeiro: "Municipal authorities in São João de Meriti, state of Rio, where a new cemetery is being planned, felt it necessary the other day to stress that the cemetery has not been officially opened so far, and would murderers therefore refrain from dumping dead bodies of victims on that site, as has frequently happened lately."

■ At the Movies

Jon Davidson, head of advertising and publicity for New World Pictures, discussing the marketing of exploitation films: "Ordinary rape and murder just doesn't make it anymore. It's much better to have ultra-violence, chain-saw massacres, X-rated Draculas, and continents sinking into the sea with the entire population lost, at the very least."

■ Wild Blue Yonder

The Air Force decided to permit members of the service to carry umbrellas, provided (1) it is raining; (2) the umbrella is black or dark blue; and (3) it is held in the left hand, to leave the right free for saluting.

■ Utility English

The National Council of Teachers of English presented its annual Doublespeak Award to the Metropolitan Edison Co., operator of the Three Mile Island nuclear plant, for coining such terms as "energetic disassembly" (explosion), "rapid oxidization" (fire) and "normal aberration" (reactor accident).

■ An Apple a Day . . .

Morticians in Bogotá, Colombia, reported that death rates declined by about a third during a protracted strike of nurses and physicians.

■ Deliberate Speed

After seventeen years of careful deliberation, the British government announced official standards for the stiffness of toothbrush bristles.

■ The Way It Crumbles

At Ocean Beach, Fire Island, New York, a young man was arrested on a charge of eating a chocolate chip cookie in public.

■ Going My Way?

From the student handbook at fundamentalist Bob Jones University, Greenville, South Carolina: "No young man may walk with a girl on campus unless both of them have a legitimate reason for going in the same direction. Couples may not invent a reason to be going the same way; they must both be going in the same direction for a definite purpose."

■ Cruel and Unusual Punishment

In Carlsbad, New Mexico, District Judge Harvey Fort sentenced a young woman to attend college while serving a term of probation for shooting her husband. It was cheaper, he said, than sending her to prison.

■ Reverse Discrimination

Oil Can Harry's Oilers, a San Francisco softball team, was barred from the second annual Gay World Series for having too many heterosexuals on its squad.

■ A Better Mousetrap

The Neiman-Marcus Christmas catalog featured a twelve-foot plastic mouse ranch, complete with corrals and fences, as a gift for anyone "who has ever dreamed of being a cattle baron." It cost $3,500, not including mice.

■ Fly Now, Pay Later

The U.S. Air Force Academy ruled that women cadets who become pregnant may remain in school—unless they get married. The academy bars married cadets.

■ Flying Turkey

Major General Charles F. Kuyk Jr. told the *Wall Street Journal* that despite many production snags, the Air Force is pleased with the C-5A cargo jet, though "having the wings fall off at 8,000 hours is a problem."

■ Much Ado . . .

The U.S. Metric Association, Inc., issued a twenty-eight-page pamphlet urging that *meter* and *liter* be spelled *metre* and *litre*.

■ Collection Plate

The Federal Communications Commission charged radio stations in Portsmouth and Norfolk (Virginia), Atlanta (Georgia) and Union City (New Jersey) with allowing religious broadcasters to provide listeners with tips on how the Lord can help them win at the numbers game.

■ Economy in Government

Every employee whose last name consists of three or fewer letters was dropped from the Department of Agriculture telephone directory.

■ Fun for the Whole Family

In Harlingen, Texas, 40,000 spectators paid up to $5 each to watch retired Air Force General Paul Tibbets re-enact the atom bombing of Hiroshima. A U.S. Army demolition team set off a simulated A-bomb, complete with mushroom cloud.

■ Laugh? I Thought I'd Die

Public protests forced a British toy manufacturer to withdraw a game called "Bombshell," which depicted a bomb-disposal squad in the process of being blown up. It had been advertised as "explosively funny for those aged six and upwards."

■ Science for the People

Soviet scientists tested public reaction to songs written by a computer against old-fashioned human music. The computer won.

■ How to Win Friends and Influence People

Robert A. Cedarburg, campaigning for Congress in St. Louis, told a senior citizens' group that providing for the elderly is a greater problem than it used to be because "fortunately, in the years past, they died at an earlier age."

■ Lost in the Stars

A World War II research report commissioned by the Roosevelt Administration and recently found in the Temple University library proposed rocketing "surplus population"—especially wartime Jewish refugees—to Venus or Mars for resettlement.

■ Tsk, Tsk, Such Manners

An executive of the Guatemalan government admitted to reporters that six political prisoners should not have been executed just before the Pope's visit: "It was a mistake. It shows a lack of politeness to kill people when the Pope asks us not to do it."

■ A Choice, Not an Echo

Paul T. Lanyhow notified the Federal Election Commission that he was running for President under an assumed name because he did not believe personalities should divert attention from the issues. His registration form arrived with no return address and seven cents postage due.

■ Awake at the Switch

Comment from John Hogan, supervisor of news information for the Commonwealth Edison Company, after a Nuclear Regulatory Commission inspector found two operators asleep on the job at the Dresden nuclear power plant near Chicago: "It depends on your definition of asleep. They weren't stretched out. They had their eyes closed. They were seated at their desks with their heads in a nodding position."

■ Not to Mention Population Control

James Chandler Bowling, senior vice president of Philip Morris, Inc., the nation's second-largest cigarette manufacturer, received the International Sanitary Supply Association's Cleaner World Award for his "major impact on making the world a cleaner and healthier place in which to live."

■ Escalation

General James H. Merryman, discussing the accuracy of today's weapons systems in an address to Army pilots: "War is becoming very lethal."

■ We Do It All for You

Professor Bruce Hannon of the University of Illinois calculated that it takes the sustained yield of more than 630 square miles of forest to provide the McDonald's hamburger chain with a year's supply of paper packaging.

■ Good News Bares

The Central Maryland chapter of the Heart Association reported, after two years of testing, that only 2 percent of the residents of the Pine Tree Association Nudist Camp had high blood pressure; among non-nudists, the rate is 15 to 20 percent.

■ Kill 'em with Kindness

Conservative philosopher Russell Kirk, reflecting on capital punishment: "Death . . . can be a friend, a mother, a lover. . . . For all of us, in the end, death is the ultimate mercy. I do not understand why we should deny that mercy to slayers whose earthly existence is a grave."

■ Now It's Official

The U.S. Treasury defines *tax* as "a compulsory payment for which no specific benefit is received in return."

■ Too, Too Divine

Phyllis Schlafly says: "The atomic bomb is a marvelous gift that was given to our country by a wise God."

■ Semper Fidelis

A Marine Corps enlisted man who applied for conscientious-objector status on religious grounds was advised by his commanding officer, "If the Marine Corps wanted you to have a god, they would have issued you one."

■ Three—Count 'em, Three— Dimensions

Finecrafted Homes Corporation, a Pacific Northwest firm, advertises: "Our artists and technology create a three-dimensional environment. . . ."

■ Copping a Plea

Steve Landesberg, who played Detective Dietrich on the *Barney Miller* television series: "Honesty is the best policy. Of course, insanity is a better defense."

■ Conversion

Featured on the jukebox in an Upper Michigan bar: *Jesus, Drop-Kick Me Through the Goalposts of Life.*

■ O Captain, My Captain

President Reagan's comment to the National Security Council when he decided not to sign the Law of the Sea Treaty, as reported by the Washington *Post*'s Lou Cannon: "We're policed and patrolled on land, and there is so much regulation, that I kind of thought that when you go out on the high seas you can do what you want."

■ Goodbye, Hello

Morgan Guaranty Trust Company of New York instructed its employees: "Avoid saying 'hello.' This elsewhere pleasant and familiar greeting is out of place in the world of business."

■ Your Tax Dollars at Work

The U.S. Food and Drug Administration has determined that pears described as "chunky" must be peeled, cored and cut into pieces at least 13 millimeters wide but not more than 44 millimeters long.

■ Wages of Sin

Dr. Henry Lyons, a psychiatrist who counsels students at the University of Florida, said premarital sex is a sign of mental illness and usually leads to suicide, drug and alcohol abuse, or promiscuity. Fortunately, he said, only a tiny percentage of his patients have engaged in the practice, and the number is dwindling.

■ Chilling Effect

A resolution offered in the Utah Legislature would have curbed the sale of ice cream because "the increased weight, lethargy, and general malaise of the adult population resulting from the increased use of heavy ice cream presents a serious threat to the very fiber of family relationships."

■ A Trip to Remember

The nuclear power industry is promoting visits to atomic plants as "mildly adventurous" additions to any vacation. At Three Mile Island, Pennsylvania, a four-color brochure advises: "A walk through the Visitors Center provides you with a close look at the work being done in Unit 2. Cleanup . . . decontamination . . . waste handling . . . all are performed with the safety of the workers and the public foremost in mind. . . . And, weather permitting, you're welcome to have your picnic lunch at the tables behind the Center. Enjoy your stay. Let us know of your questions or concerns. We're here to help you."

■ Can't Hack It

Former South Vietnamese Premier Nguyen Cao Ky said he abandoned plans to become a taxicab driver in the United States because it is a "rough life" and "you have to know the syndicate."

■ A Grip on Reality

According to an ad in *Business Week,* "REALITY and ENGLISH are registered trademarks of Microdata Corporation, Irvine, CA."

■ Death and Taxes

Representative James R. Jones, Oklahoma Democrat, said some of his constituents "have been waiting three or four years to die" because Congress took so long to revise the inheritance tax laws.

■ Someplace to Hide

Marc Hacker, an architecture student at Princeton University, designed an underground fallout shelter large enough to house 30,000 people. It would be built under Coyote Springs, Nevada, where the Air Force proposed putting an MX missile complex.

■ It's a Big, Big Country

Defense Secretary Caspar Weinberger said one reason for
continued U.S. aid to El Salvador is that it "is on the
mainland of the United States, and we do have a responsibility
for the defense of the continental United States, over and
above all other priorities."

■ No Rugelach for Rover

Remco, a New York novelty-item manufacturer, said
lukewarm consumer response made it necessary to shelve
plans for marketing Mother Klein's Kosher-Style Dog Food.

■ The Faithful Dead

More than a year after he died, Rufus Owen Watts Sr. was
re-elected to the Democratic Committee in Halifax, Virginia.
County Chairman Howard P. Anderson explained that the party
had a policy of "not dumping" members who serve faithfully.

■ Frontiers of Free Enterprise

Pookki Designs of Encinitas, California, advertised a "Chi Energy Shirt" that "utilizes oriental acupressure and color system" to "increase meridian energy flow, balance glandular function, and protect against environmental stress."

■ Reach for a Roscoe Instead of a Book

Montgomery County Junior College in Blue Bell, Pennsylvania, citing "a lack of demonstrated interest," shut down its library science program and replaced it with a lethal-weapons training course.

■ Frontiers of Religion

The Universal Life Church of Sunnyvale, California, installed a computer called "Rev. Apple" to perform marriage ceremonies. The human co-celebrant, the Reverend Reinhard Jaenisch, said, "I'm into making church fun."

■ No Place to Hide

A Texas state legislator, Representative Ron Waters, introduced a bill that would require utilities to store their nuclear wastes in their corporate executive suites.

■ Loaves and Fishes

Joan Cavanaugh, author of *More of Jesus, Less of Me,* told participants in a Los Angeles workshop on "Christian Weight Control" to shun "Satan's food" and "only buy foods that Jesus, John or Peter would buy."

■ Straight to the Top

The Church of God in Commack, New York, received a fund-raising letter from President Reagan, seeking a $120 contribution "to keep Republican Senators in office." It began, "Dear Mr. God."

■ Potemkin Air Bases

The West German magazine *Stern* claimed the Soviet Union has been fooling U.S. spy satellites by building fake air bases out of cardboard.

■ Looking at the Bright Side

From the annual report of Forum Group, Inc., a corporation that once sold auto body parts and now operates hospitals: "Today's pressured life style" and "the breakdown of traditional family values" ensure a continuing rise in drug abuse and emotional problems, so that "we have the opportunity to grow in revenues and earnings beyond the fondest dreams of most managements."

■ Newspeak

A report by the President's Commission on Pension Policy referred to persons aged sixty-five and over as "aged units."

■ Boys Won't Be Boys

Topic of a discussion program at a community health center in Madison, Wisconsin: "Circumcision—A Health Care Issue for Baby Men."

■ Penal Reform

Philip Weber, Republican counsel to the Illinois State Senate and a member of the Illinois Bar Association's prison reform committee, offered two plans for relieving prison crowding and making streets safer: (1) put violent criminals into a drug-induced coma for the duration of their terms; and (2) release nonviolent offenders into the community, provided they wear Day-Glo orange uniforms and shaved heads. "I'm serious," Weber said.

■ Say What, Cap'n?

Excerpt from a U.S. Navy briefing: "The absence of fully programming to these enlisted manpower requirements without a concomitant reduction in either ship capability requirements or endurance parameters forms a dichotomy between our stated mission/objectives and the individual unit's ability to carry out the stated mission in peacetime environment."

■ New Hope for the Peaceful Atom . . .

Joe Vogler, the Alaskan Independence Party's unsuccessful candidate for governor, urged the use of nuclear bombs to blast a path through glaciers for construction of a coastal highway from Seattle to Alaska.

■ Sex and the Senator

Senator Jeremiah Denton, Alabama Republican, opposing legislation that would permit prosecution of a husband for raping his wife: "When you get married you might expect you're going to get a little sex."

■ Win This One for the Gipper

"The Kingdom of Heaven is like a football squad, which is assembled under
a coach who formed it into a team that moved with such order and
precision, in startling innovation, that it subdued all its opponents."
—From a sermon delivered in the football stadium at Notre Dame
University by the Reverend Larry Christenson of San Pedro, California.

■ Love and Money

Armand Hammer, whose Occidental Petroleum empire includes
Hooker Chemical, the company that dumped carcinogenic wastes at
Love Canal, established a $1 million prize for the scientist who finds a
cure for cancer.

■ Jes' Folks

According to the *Bottom Line,* the newspaper published by Columbia University's
Business School, "There are, in fact, very few ways in which corporations
absolutely differ from people, if we set anatomy aside for the moment."

■ Unthinkable

South African Justice Minister James T. Kruger warned Parliament
that if the country were to repeal its miscegenation laws,
the result would be "people who can vote and love and live together."

■ I ♥ Khartoum

According to the *Times* of London, the Sudanese government
moved prostitutes out of the red-light district of Khartoum
and into the suburbs "as part of a plan to reorganize and
beautify the Sudanese capital."

■ All the Comforts of Home

Marc Leeds, vice president of the American Pet Motel in the Chicago
suburbs, said the establishment's clientele of 10,000 animal borders a
year included "a cat who drinks chocolate milk and a Chihuahua who
gets a bowl of Pepsi with four ice cubes and has ham and eggs for
breakfast and steak for lunch."

■ A Dog's Life

An airborne corps spokesman at Fort Bragg, North Carolina, explaining why the Army contemplates only limited use of parachuting dogs: "We have soldiers here in training jumping every day, but we wouldn't consider jumping the dogs that often. It's an expensive proposition to train the dogs, and we don't want to take unnecessary risks with them."

■ The Silent Majority Speaks

In Ward, Colorado, John Farley was elected mayor several weeks after he died of pneumonia. A friend explained, "Ward's a ghost town, and we decided to elect a dead man to represent the silent majority."

■ Beautification

The Pennsylvania Legislature voted to add the term "automotive dismantler and recycler" to the state statutes. It replaces the word "junkyard."

■ Boom Times Ahead

News story in the *Wellsboro Gazette,* Tioga County, Pennsylvania: "A nuclear war could be the best thing to happen in Tioga County in these depressed economic times. If the Federal Government has planned accordingly and if local businessmen are prepared, Tioga County can enjoy the biggest boom in its history when 115,000 New Jersey residents motor in and register at Mansfield State College, hopefully in time for supper at one of the 217 feeding facilities capable of providing 71,300 meals at one time. . . ."

■ Top-Floor Vacancy

From the "Manager's Journal" column in the
Wall Street Journal: "Top managers must learn
to cultivate ignorance. The higher you go, the
less you really should know about what is actually
going on."

■ Genetic Defect

The Reverend Billy James Hargis, founder of the Crusade for Christian Morality and the American Christian College in Tulsa, Oklahoma, said "genes and chromosomes" drove him to illicit sexual relations with male and female students.

■ Are You Listening, Reverend Hargis?

Minnesota State Representative John Spanish, commenting on a bill to permit vending-machine sales of contraceptives, said the legislation would not be needed "if people would just learn to keep their pants zipped up."

■ Know Your Enemy

The U.S. Commerce Department told the Mennonite Central Committee that it may not send notebooks, pencils, erasers and rulers to Cambodian schoolchildren because that would constitute "developmental aid" to the Vietnamese-backed Cambodian government, which the United States does not recognize.

■ Family Assistance Plan

From a news release issued by Monsieur Henri
Wines, Ltd., in response to demands for a boycott
of imports from the Soviet Union: "We are *not*
backing Russia in their actions, nor are we
promoting Russia by marketing Stolichnaya
vodka. We are simply promoting a very saleable,
imported vodka that helps numerous American
families and has the backing of the United States
Government."

■ Admirals First

When U.S. Coast Guard headquarters in Washington received a bomb threat, eight admirals were immediately evacuated. The other 2,000 civilian and military Coast Guard employees weren't even told.

■ Draw Your Own Inference

From an arms control impact statement submitted to Congress by the Pentagon under terms of the Arms Control and Disarmament Act: "The [deleted] is a key element of the Worldwide Military Command and Control System (WWMCCS) warning network. . . . [Deleted] currently consists of [deleted] satellite; two [deleted] satellites; an [deleted] for [deleted] from the [deleted] satellite; a [deleted] for [deleted] and the [deleted] satellites; and a [deleted] which provides [deleted] for the [deleted]. . . . Using these data, [deleted] can be inferred."

■ Civics Lesson

House Speaker Tip O'Neill, explaining why Congress granted itself a pay raise without voting on the issue: "There are instances where it is in the best interests of the nation not to vote the will of the people."

■ Look for the Silver Lining

The *Wall Street Journal*, reporting on the failure of two (out of two) operational flight tests of the cruise missile: "The Air Force doesn't call the tests 'failures,' preferring to call them 'partial successes' because the missiles worked 'flawlessly' until they went off course."

■ The Real Thing

An announcement from the Alamo Consulting Group: "The Alamo Consulting Group leads the field of management development in proactive processes with a new validated design. The Process Management Skills Program is criterion-referenced, assuring effectiveness and efficiency of the varied modes of learning and relevant practice. The ultimate validation is application of the processes to real-world performance requirements, and PMS works!"

■ There You Go Again

John McManus, public relations director of the John Birch Society, told the Associated Press that Ronald Reagan is a "second-echelon member" of the Communist conspiracy.

■ The Healing Arts

The *New England Journal of Medicine* reported that of 815 consecutive patients admitted to a Boston University Medical Center ward, more than a third developed an illness or disability as a result of hospitalization, and in sixteen cases the illness or disability proved fatal.

■ There Will Be a Final Exam

Adult evening courses offered by the Danbury,
Connecticut, public schools (at $30 each) include
Astrology, Basic Upholstery, Cake Decorating,
Chair Caning and Surviving Nuclear War.

■ Learning Can Be Fun

Chemical and Engineering News reported on "a novel means for coaxing [chemistry] students through the drill work that many require for mastering this discipline"—a computer game called Nuclear Casino: "Two students try to outwit one another by answering problems spelled out on the screen. Depending on how well they answer questions about radioactive elements, each student's simulated stock of plutonium either grows or adds to the growth of his or her opponent until one of them reaches 'critical mass' and thus loses in an explosion of light."

■ Splash

Former President Gerald R. Ford was named the first honorary member of the International Swimming Hall of Fame.

■ It Can't Happen Here

The agony inflicted on the Swedish people by their government's "deepening socialism"—as recorded in the *Sentinel Star* of Orlando, Florida: ". . . their initiative has been sapped by free medical care, child care, education, low-cost housing, and countless other benefits."

■ Tax Shelter

Under the heading of "Emergency Relocation Planning and Operations," the *Internal Revenue Service Handbook* advises: "During state of national emergency resulting from enemy attack, the essential functions of the Service will be as follows: (1) assessing, collecting, and recording taxes. . . ."

■ Not to Worry

Because of a computer error, more than forty Pennsylvania counties received official warning that a nuclear attack was imminent. Nobody paid any attention.